DATE DUE

JUN 2 4 1991			
AUG 1982			
AUG 5 1986			
FEB 1 1980			
MAR 0 5 198			

J
796.342
SMI

Smith, Jay H
Fiery tennis star, Jimmy Connors

JIMMY CONNORS

PHOTO CREDITS
All photos by Bruce Curtis

Published by Creative Educational Society, Inc.,
123 South Broad Street, Mankato, Minnesota 56001
Copyright© 1977 by Creative Educational Society, Inc. International
copyrights reserved in all countries.
No part of this book may be reproduced in any form without written
permission from the publisher. Printed in the United States.

Library of Congress Cataloging in Publication Data
Smith, Jay H.
Fiery tennis star, Jimmy Connors.
SUMMARY: A brief biography of the controversial tennis star.
1. Connors, Jimmy, 1952-   —Juvenile literature.
2. Tennis players—United States—Biography—Juvenile literature.
[1. Connors, Jimmy, 1952-   2. Tennis players] I. Title.
GV994.C66S54   796.34'2'0924 [B] [92]   76-44497   ISBN 0-87191-587-1

FIERY TENNIS STAR JIMMY CONNORS

BY JAY H. SMITH

CREATIVE EDUCATION/CHILDRENS PRESS

4

The summer of 1973 was almost over. Nature was already at work. Slowly, leaf by leaf, the trees were beginning to change to bright gold and fiery red. Change was taking place in the world of tennis, too. The attention of the fans had begun to shift from the older, more famous players to a bright and fiery new star named Jimmy Connors.

6

Most fans had not yet seen Jimmy play, but they had heard a lot about him. They had heard about his brilliant groundstrokes, especially his two-fisted backhand. The top pros had tried to overpower Jimmy. But the harder they hit the ball at him, the harder he hit it back.

8

People were also talking about Jimmy's amazing speed. Racing all over the court, he was able to return balls that most players could not even reach.

CU
The U.S. OPEN is part of the
Commercial Union Grand
CU
CU

10

Everybody predicted a great future for
21-year-old Jimmy. Some people said that he would
reach the top of the tennis world as easily as he
reached for balls hit over his head.

PEN is part of t
Union Grand ix

And those people were right. Before 1974 was over, Jimmy was the very best player in the world. At the end of almost every tournament he entered, Jimmy was there to receive the winner's trophy.

14

In the summer of 1974 Jimmy went to England and won Wimbledon, the most important championship in the world. Then he returned to America and won the U.S. Open. But these triumphs did not bring Jimmy the popularity he felt he deserved. The more the fans had seen him, the less they liked him.

Jimmy would often delay the action and get in long arguments with the officials or the spectators. At times he would scream foul language at the crowd or insult his opponent. Sometimes he would make vulgar gestures or spit on the court in disgust. Most of Jimmy's fans soon grew tired of his bad manners.

18

Jimmy didn't really like being disliked. So at times he made an effort to control his temper and mind his manners. He would try to make the crowd feel happy. But he wasn't very good at it. Whenever he began to clown around, hardly anyone laughed — except Jimmy himself. He tried to be a showman and ended up looking like a show-off.

20

Jimmy didn't want to be thought of as a poor sport. Often he tried hard to be gracious. But as usual, he tried too hard. When he praised an opponent, Jimmy meant it. But the trouble was, he *sounded* insincere. It seemed strange to many people that Jimmy had so much style as a player and so little style as a man.

22

A few people began to feel sympathetic toward Jimmy. "He's a good kid, whatever you think," insisted one writer. Another reporter wrote: "Jimmy Connors is a victim of the people who run his career. They have never let him make a decision on his own. . . . Jimmy won't grow up until he has broken through the invisible shell his advisors have built around him."

24

Early in 1975, the shell seemed to close tighter
around Jimmy. The crowds greeted him with boos
wherever he played. Jimmy often reacted by flying
into a rage. When most pros get angry, they lose their
concentration. They forget basic things that every
beginner should remember. They take their eyes off
the ball. They don't bend their knees. But when
Jimmy became angry, he concentrated even harder.

And Jimmy kept on winning. He made a lot of money in two famous challenge matches in Las Vegas. There he scored impressive wins over Rod Laver and John Newcombe. That summer Jimmy left for England to defend his Wimbledon crown. He had not been beaten all year. And he looked unbeatable, reaching the Wimbledon finals easily. Then he faced Arthur Ashe, one of the most popular and respected players in tennis.

28

The fans wanted to see Jimmy blasted off the court. But Arthur knew that Jimmy's great return of serve made that impossible. In three previous matches, he had tried to overpower Jimmy and failed. Arthur decided to change his strategy. The new strategy worked. Arthur's slow, floating returns kept Jimmy off balance constantly. His delicate lobs fooled Jimmy again and again. When it was all over, Jimmy had received the beating of his life.

Losing hurt Jimmy, but it also seemed to help him. Slowly, he began to change. The shell was starting to crack.

The fans began to notice the change in Jimmy's behavior at the 1975 U.S. Open. In his first six matches, Jimmy showed he was a gracious winner. And when he lost to Manuel Orantes in the finals, Jimmy proved he was a gracious loser as well. When he praised Manuel's brilliant performance, no one doubted Jimmy's sincerity any more. There was warm applause for the fiery young tennis star that day.

BILLIE JEAN KING
O. J. SIMPSON
EVEL KNIEVEL
HANK AARON
JOE NAMATH
OLGA KORBUT
FRAN TARKENTON
MUHAMMAD ALI
CHRIS EVERT
FRANCO HARRIS
BOBBY ORR
KAREEM ABDUL JABBAR
JACK NICKLAUS
JOHNNY BENCH
JIMMY CONNORS
A. J. FOYT

THE ALLSTARS